Remnant Words of the Boricua Indian

© 2020 Richard Morrow Porrata Doria, Ph.D.
ISBN 9781656331151

All rights reserved. No portion of this publication may be reproduced, distributed or transmitted in any form or by any means, including photocopying, recording or other electronic or mechanical methods without written permission.

Cover Art: By Author
Interior Art: By Author

Format: American Psychological Association (APA)

Yukibo Books
Isabela, Puerto Rico
www.yukibobooks.com
fb.me/yukibobooks

Author Since 1989

Table of Contents

Dedication	iv
Introduction	v
Taino Dictionary	1
Bibliography	28

Dedication

In memory of Taino Chief Rosa Morales.

Yukibo

Introduction

    I have put this simple book together as a means not only to preserve words and phrases of the Taino language but also for those practitioners of the Taino language who might be missing words that can help them fill in the blanks when trying to formulate sentences in this Native American language. It has been my deepest ambition for nearly 30 years to restore this ancestral language of my mother's Taino ancestors. Interesting enough, through Church records and vital statistics from Puerto Rico, her family's oral history of a Taino heritage back to the Indiera was proven along with discovering a great-grand father who served in the Four Companies of Indian Soldiers from the San German Urban Militia (Cardona Bonet, 1817). As a note, and a bit off tangent, many Puerto Ricans are not aware that Puerto Rico had an Indian militia under the command of the Spanish army that was stationed in San German. Furthermore, many Puerto Ricans are also not aware that vintage vital statistics are housed in municipality demographic offices across Puerto Rico that identify some Puerto Rican ancestors as *indio* (Indian). For more information on how one can discover and prove their Taino roots via a paper trail, they might want to read my book <u>Taino Genealogy and Revitalization</u>. This book gives in-depth instruction on how a person who has a Taino family oral history can do the same research as I have done proving there is absolutely no denial of their Taino heritage. Therefore, making it my hope that they as well as I have been, are inspired to learn their native ancestral language even if they only learn its simplest form. For those who would like to learn more of the Taino language at an intermediate or advanced level there is the fairytale <u>Chin Kori</u> and <u>Keeping the Taino Language Alive; Advanced Studies in Taino Syntax</u>. <u>Chin Kori</u> teaches the reader how to use simple present and past tense forms in Taino; plus it has a meaningful message for both children and adults. <u>Keeping the Taino Language Alive; Advanced Studies in Taino Syntax</u> describes how to construct Taino sentences not only in the present and simple past tense but also in the present continuous tense, past continuous tense, past perfect tense, future simple tense, future perfect tense and perfect tense. This book also describes how the Taino verb *toka*, which in English is the verb *to be* and in Spanish is the verb *ser/estar*, is properly conjugated. Moreover, the book is full of Taino prefixes and suffixes with many examples of Taino sentences that the practitioner can use as models to form his or her own Taino sentences. It has taken me close to 30 years to unravel much of the Taino language. Fortunately God gave me the tools to put much of its syntax together from gaining experience as a language professor at the University of Puerto Rico's Multilingual and Cultural Institute Division of Continuing Education, and as a language instructor for the United States Army. Additionally, adding to my doctorate degree in philosophy, I acquired 120 credit hours in Native American linguistics from the University of Oregon, where I learned many techniques toward awakening the Taino language.

    Returning back to my mother's maternal side is a paper trail recorded as far back as 1785, with direct family ancestors who resided in the Indiera. The Indiera was a Taino community where Taino people lived isolated from the Spaniards. In essence, this was Puerto Rico's Indian reservation where many of the words illustrated in this book were found, and which some are still being creolized into the Spanish language throughout Puerto Rico's Central Mountain Range. This is where many Taino people resided for hundreds of years since their release from slavery in 1542 by their Spanish oppressors (Brau, 1881). However, as each generation passes Taino words pass with them and can be forever lost, which makes this book so important. Some of the words in this book are found in other books as <u>Clásicos de Puerto Rico</u> by Coll and Toste, <u>Diccionario de Voces Indígenas de Puerto Rico</u> by Luis Hernández Aquino, and <u>Languages of the Pre-Columbian Antilles</u> by Julian Granberry and Gary S. Vescelius. However, what makes this book unique are the many remnant words of the Taino language that are not found in any other linguistic book of this Native American language but only from the Boricua country side; Boricua being the true name of the Taino Indians of Puerto Rico.

It is believed by many that the Taino language is extinct but there is some literature and testimonies that point to a few pockets of people who were still speaking it within the last 150 years or so (Hernández Aquino, 1977). Fortunately, someone years ago recorded these remnant words given to them by an old Taino woman from the mountain community of Maricao where the Indiera is found. This is how it was told to me by Taino Chief Rosa Morales who gave me the list of words. She had become very fond of me in a motherly way and even appointed me as Ambassador of the Taino People of Boriken (Taino name for the island of Puerto Rico) where I represented the Taino people when visiting other tribes in the Continental United States as the Shawnees, Cherokees, and Navajos for example. She later appointed me as her deputy chief and I was given the Taino name *Yukibo*, through a Taino ceremony. Moreover, the 1990's was an era in which great things occurred for me such as becoming a deputy chief in the Caribe Indian Nation under Paramount Chief Hilary Frederick on the island of Dominica. Additionally, I became the President of the Native American and Alaskan Native Coalition where I represented a coalition of Native American federal employees. It was an honor for me to hold these prestigious positions within the Native American community and I will always be grateful that I was given these opportunities which enriched my self-awareness of my own American Indian heritage. In turn however, it has forced me to push myself harder in honor of my Taino ancestors toward researching and publishing all that I have discovered about my gained knowledge of their language. It is sharing with others what I have discovered about awaking the Taino language that brings me great joy! However, our Creator and Lord works in mysterious ways because if I had never known Chief Rosa Morales, I might not have ever taken an interest towards putting the pieces to the puzzle together towards awakening this language.

Who originally recorded the words in this book and who the old Indian woman was, I do not know and may never know. Therefore, the author is unknown but the list is very old because when it was given to me by Chief Morales, most people didn't have a word-processor and if you analyze the writing you can tell that a type writer was used. For how many years Chief Morales had this list of Taino words I do not know this either but she spoke of the old Taino woman as though she knew her when she herself was a young lady. At the time I knew Chief Morales she was up in age and I was a young man. So it is my impression that the old Taino woman she spoke of was born sometime in the 1800's. I only wish that when Chief Morales gave me the list I had been more attentive to ask her who interviewed the old Taino lady towards acquiring these words and to have known more about this woman. It could be that it was Chief Morales herself who interviewed the old Taino woman and recorded these words. Unfortunately, Chief Morales has long passed so it will undoubtedly remain a mystery. Thus, I have taken it upon myself to publish these words so that they are forever recorded and available to others who wish to add more words to their Taino vocabulary. Interestingly, as a child I heard my mother using some of these words. However, it wouldn't be until years later as an adult, that I discovered that she was using Taino words. I just assumed they were Spanish words not realizing that the Spanish language in Puerto Rico had been creolized with Taino words, especially in the central mountain region.

As you examine these Taino words please note that some of the words may have a letter that has been underlined. The line under the letter represents that the letter is accented; therefore, giving the same accented sound as is found in the Spanish language (i.e. a = á). Also, the Taino vowel sounds are the same vowel sounds found in the Spanish language. Therefore, for those who speak Spanish they will find it easy to pronounce these Taino words. Moreover, consonants in the Taino

Taino vowel sounds are the same as Spanish vowel sounds		
a	/a/ = a	father
e	/e/ = eh	day
i	/i/ = ee	machine
o	/o/ = oh	go
u	/u/ = oo	goose

language are pronounced the same as consonants found in both English and Spanish. Thus, this makes it easier to pronounce Taino words for those people who speak English or Spanish. However, please note that the two exceptions are that *h* is silent in Spanish and that *j* is pronounced as *h* in Spanish. Furthermore, Taino words having *ch* sounds have the same or similar *ch* sounds found in both English and Spanish. Unlike other Native American languages we are lucky that the Taino language has these similarities with the English and Spanish languages.

I hope you find this Taino word list interesting and valuable, and that you become as enthusiastic as I have been towards learning this beautiful American Indian language. Best wishes always and have a blessed day.

Taí guéi,

Yukibo

Remnant Words of the Boricua Indian

LA LETRA "A":

A	SEMEJANTE/DOBLE, IGUAL	SIMILAR, DOUBLE/THE SAME
ABA	ABICHUELA/GRANO	BEAN
ABARA(BARA)	PELO/CABELLO	HAIR
ABATIMAN	# SEIS (6)	# SIX (6)
ABE	OTROS	OTHERS
ABO	OTRO	ANOTHER
ABO	SITIO DONDE HAY AGUA	PLACE WHERE THERE'S WATER
ABON	CORRIENTE	CURRENT
ACHIANO	ESTRELLA DEL SUR, ABUELA DEL SUR	STAR OF THE GRANDMOTHER OF THE SOUTH
ASIGUATAQ	TRISTE/DEBIL	SAD/WEAK
ADA	ARBOL	TREE
ADDALIA	SALIR/SURGIR	TO COME OUT, TO ARISE
ADKABUKO(AIDKABUKO) (ARKABUKO)	VOSQUE	FOREST
AHAU	REDONDO	CIRCULAR
AHI	PIMIENTA	PEPPER
AI	DIENTE	TOOTH
AIAKA	TAMALE DE MAIZ	CORN TAMALE
AIAN	HABLAR/DECIR/CONTAR, DIRIGIRSE A UNO	TO SAY/TO TELL/TO SPEAK/TO ADDRESS ONE-SELF
AIANA	VOZ	VOICE
AIANI(AINI)	AGITADO/ALBOROTOSO, VOZ ALTA	AGITATED, LOUD/TO CALL OUT
AIBKO	CIRCULO	CIRCLE
AIDIMAR(YARIMA) (ARIMA)	ANO	ANUS
AIDIMARA	ESPALDA	BACK TEETH
AII	LENGUA	TONGUE
AITE	LLENO DE DIENTES	FILLED WITH TEETH
AITINAL	POSTE DE CASA	HOUSE POLE
AKO(KAKO)	OJO/VER	EYE/TO SEE
AMAKA	AMACA	HAMOCK
AMOKA	# DOS (2)	# TWO (2)
ANAKE	POR QUE?	WHY?
ANAKI(ANKI)	ENEMIGO	ENEMY
ANAMA	ESPERANZA	HOPE
ANANA	PINA	PINEAPPLE

Taíno	Español	English
ANAO(ANA)	FLOR/SURGIR/BROTAR, NACER/BOCA DE RIO	FLOWER/TO SPROUT/TO BUD/TO BE BORN/RIVER'S MOUTH
ANTI	REDUCIR/MAS PEQUEÑO	REDUCED, SMALLER
AON(ALKO)	PERRO	DOG
APITO	COSA INFINITA/SIN PRINCIPIO O FIN	ENDLESS THING, WITHOUT BEGGING OR END
ARA(IARA)	SITIO/LUGAR	A PLACE
ARAGUAKA	DANZA	A DANCE
ARASIBO	SITIO PEDREGOSO	A PLACE WITH MANY STONES
AREIBO	CUENTO/LEYENDA	STORY/LEGEND
AREITO	CANTAR/RITO CON CANTO Y BAILA	TO SING, RITUAL WITH SONG & DANCING
AREITO BI(RAREITO)	ARMONIA	HARMONY
AREITO DI	CEREMONIA	CEREMONY
AREITO HARA	DEMANDAR	DEMAND
AREITO TI	ORAR/ORACION, ROGAR/PEDIR PARA	PRAY/PRAYER BEG/ASK FOR
ARI	DIA	DAY
ARIIUNA	EXTRANJERO	FOREIGNER
ARKABUKO	MONTE ESPESO CERRADO POR MALESA	THICK MOUNTAIN COVER BY UNDERBRUSH
AROKOEL(KAROKOI) (KAROTOI) (KOROTI) (OKOROTI)	ABUELO	GRANDFATHER
ASI	CABESA	HEAD
ATA(BIBI/TOA)	MADRE/DIOSA	MOTHER, GODDESS
ATA BARIBAKOA	CLAN	CLAN
ATABEI(ATABEX) (ATTABEIRA)	MADRE TIERRA, MADRE DEL COSMO	MOTHER EARTH COSMIC MOTHER
ATAKAN(ATIKE,ATAKE) (ATIKEN,ARIKE)	OREJA	EAR
ATIAO	AMIGO/CAMARADA	FRIEND, COMRADE
ATO	ESTADO O CONDICION DE UNA PERSONA	STATE OR CONDITION OF A PERSON
ATO	DULCE	SWEET
ATRATA	MADRE DEL CLAN	CLAN MOTHER
AUIAMA	CALABASA	PUMPKIN, SQUASH

AUMAGUA	PUESTO/ENCIMA/ARRIBA	ON/OVER/UP
AUNA	AL FRENTE/ADELANTE, DELANTERO	BEFORE/FORTH FOWARD
AUNAGUA	BAJO/DE BAJO	DOWN/UNDER
AUPAGUA	ADENTRO/DENTRO	INSIDE/IN
AURA	BUITRE	VULTURE
AURAGUA	AFUERA/FUERA	OUTSIDE/OUT
AUSAGUA	AL LADO	BESIDE
AUTAGUA	AL OTRO LADO DE	ACROSS
AIAKA	AREPAS	CORN MEAL ROLES WITH BEEF INSIDE

LA LETRA "B":

BA	TENER/POSEER	TO HAVE/TO POSSESS
BABA	PADRE/PAPA	FATHER/DAD
BABAE(BABEY)	SUMBADOR	HUMMING BIRD
BABERONI	VASIJA DE HIGUERA CON AGUA	GORE VESSEL WITH WATER
BABINEI	FANGAL/LODAZAL	MUDDY PLACE, MUDHOLE
BADA	UNA/GARRA	NAIL/CLAW
BAGUA ABON	ARROYO	BROOK/STREAM
BAGUA BO	EL MAR	THE SEA
BAGUA KATO	LAGO	LAKE
BAGUA LI	RIO	RIVER
BAHAKU(BAJAKU)	LUCERO DE LA MANANA	MORNING LIGHT
BAHARAKE(BAJARAKE)	CASA GRANDE	LARGE HOUSE
BAHARI(BAJARI)	SENOR/TRATAMIENTO DE RESPETO/TERCER EN RANGO DEL JEFE	LORD/TREATMENT OF RESPECT, THIRD FROM THE CHIEF
BAI	A YI/ESOS	THERE/THAT
BAIGUN	RED DE PESCAR	FISHING NET
BAIOIA	LAGARTO	LIZARD
BAIRA(SIMARABO)	ARCO DE FLECHA	BOW
BAMA	PAPA GRANDE	BIG FATHER
BAN	AVE/PAJARO	BIRD
BANA	YA	ALREADY, RIGHT AWAY
BANEKE	POR QUE TU?	WHY YOU?
BARAKUTA(BARAKUTEY)	UN AVE SOLA	A LONE BIRD
BARI	FAMILIA	FAMILY
BARIBA KOA(BARBAKOA)	HOGAR/HOGUERA, CARRUAJE PARA UNA FOGATA/UNA CASA PARA SECAR CARNE O TABACO	HEARTH/HOME, FIRE PLACE, RIG OF POLES FOR A CAMP FIRE/A HOUSE TO DRY MEAT

BAT<u>E</u>A	ATRAVES O CACEROLA GRANDE O PALANGANA GRANDE	OR TABACO THROUGH OR LARGE PAN OR LARGE BOWL
BAT<u>E</u>I	PATIO/PLAZA, SITIO DE JUEGO	BACK YARD, SQUARE/A PLACE WARE BALL IS PLAY
BAT<u>OS</u>(BAT<u>U</u>)	PELOTA/JUEGO CEREMONIAL	BALL/CEREMONIAL GAME
B<u>A</u>IA(B<u>A</u>YA)	PLANTA	PLANT
BA<u>I</u>O<u>I</u>A(BAY<u>O</u>YA)	LAGARTO DE COSTA	COSTAL LIZARD
BEHUKO	ENREDADERA	VINE
BEI<u>A</u>KO	MALVADO/PERSONA MALA, BRIBON/PICARO	VILLAIN/EVIL PERSON/ROGUE
BE<u>I</u>RA	EXISTENCIA/SER	EXISTENCE, TO BE
BEKET<u>I</u>(JEKET<u>I</u>)	# UNO (1)	# ONE (1)
BI	COMIENSO/PRICIPIO	BEGINING
BIBAGUA	LAGUNA DE AGUA SALADA	SALTY POND
BIBIH<u>A</u>GUA,	HORMIGA	ANT
B<u>I</u>HA(<u>B</u>IJA)	ACHIOTE	ACHIOTE
BIH<u>A</u>O(BIJAO)	HILO PARA CANASTOS, Y PARA CUBRIR CASA	STRING FOR BASKETS AND COVER HOUSES
BIM<u>I</u>NI	FUENTE DE VIDA	FOUNTAIN OF LIFE
BI<u>O</u>IA	CRECER	GROW
BO	GRANDUOSO/ALTO	GREAT/LARGE/TALL
BO BO	MAS GRANDE	LARGEST, BIGGEST
B<u>O</u>A(B<u>O</u>BA)	CULEBRA	SNAKE
B<u>O</u>ANI	PROSPERAR/MEJORAR	THRIVE/TO DO WELL
BOGUA	VIVIR/RESIDIR/VIVO, VIDA	LIVE/TO LIVE TO RESIDE, LIFE
BOE<u>I</u>ERI	ADULTO	ADULT
BOI BOGUN	NACIMIENTO	BIRTH
B<u>O</u>INAN	LUZ DE SOL	SUN LIGHT
B<u>O</u>INAEL	EL SOL	THE SUN
B<u>O</u>I<u>O</u>	CASA	HOUSE
B<u>O</u>I<u>O</u>	ORGANOS GENITALES DE LA MUJER	FEMALE GENITALS
B<u>O</u>IO BAI	EL BIENTRE/UTERO	WOMB
B<u>O</u>IOTA	EMBARASADA/PRENADA	PREGNANT
BOITI<u>O</u>(BOIKE)(BEIKE)	SACERDOTE	SHAMAN
BO MATUM	GRAN GENEROSIDAD (GRACIAS)	GREAT GENEROSITY (THANK YOU)
BON<u>I</u>ATO	BATATA	SWEET POTATO
B<u>O</u>RIA	LABOR	LABOR

BOR**I**KEN	TIERRA DEL SENOR NOBLE/VALIENTE	LAND OF THE VALIANT, NOBLE LORD
BOR**I**KUA	PERSONA NOBLE	NOBLE PERSON
BOS**I**BA	PIEDRA GRANDE	LARGE STONE
B**U**	COLOR	COLOR
B**U**ALI	COLORADO/ROJO	RED
B**U**ANI	ANARANJADO/CHINITA	ORANGE
B**U**BE	BLANCO	WHITE
B**U**KAN	PARRILLA PARA ASAR	GRILL TO COOK ON
B**U**ELI	AMARILLO	YELLOW
B**U**ENI	VERDE	GREEN
B**U**INI	PURPURA	PURPLE
B**U**ITI	AZUL	BLUE
B**U**ITIKAKO(BUITIAKO)	OJOS NEGROS	BLACK EYES
B**U**MA	NEGRO	BLACK
B**U**NA	MARRON	BROWN
B**U**REN	PIESA DONDO SE MAJABA EL MAIS	GRIDDLE
BUR**I**KEDAN	AMASAR/MESCLAR	BLEND/MIX
BUR**U**KENA	CANGREJO DE AGUA DULCE	SWEET WATER CRAB
BUSAO	REGALO	GIFT
BUS**I**KA	DAR/PROVEER/COMUNICAR, TRANSPORTAR	TO GIVE/TO PROVIDE/TO CONVEY
BUT**A**KA	ASIENTO	SEAT
BUT**A**M	OSCURO	DARK

EL SONIDO "CH":

CHIN CHIN	MUY PEQUENO	VERY LITTLE
CHIPOHO	LAGARTO	LIZARD
CHIPOHO BO	DRAGON/MONSTRO	DRAGON, MONSTER
CHORETO	MUY ABUNDANTE	VERY ABUNDANT
CHUK CHUK	CASCABELES	JINGLE BELLS

LA LETRA "D":

DA	MIO(A)/MI	MY/ME
DA B**A**RA	MI PELO/CABELLO	MY HAIR
D**A**HLIA	FLOR USADA COMO ORNAMENTO	FLOWER USED AS ORNAMENT
DAI	AQUI	HERE
D**A**IN	ESTO(A)	THIS
DA K**A**BO	MI MANO	MY HAND
DAK**I**A(DAKA)	YO	I/ME
DA K**U**TI	MI PIES	MY FOOT
D**A**NA	PIERNA	PIERNA
D**A**TIHAO	MI SENOR/MI AMIGO	MY LORD,

		MY FRIEND
DATTI	MI PADRE	MY FATHER
DENA	BRASO	ARM
DENAN	HOMBRO	SHOULDER
DIGO	AZUL DE AÑIL	INDIGO
DITA	COPA/PLATO/PALANGANA, CUCHARON HECHO DE DE HIGUERA	CUP/PLATE, BOWL/DIPPER MADE OF GORE
DITE	HIJO	SON
DUHO(DUJO)	BANCO/TRONO/SILLA	BENCH/STOOL, THRONE
DUIAN	ROMPER	BREAK
DUHA(DUJA)	CORTAR	CUT

FRASES-PHRASES:

DAKIA IERA GUARIKO DAI = "I DID COME"
DAKIA IERE GUARIKO DAI = "I DO COME"
DAKIA IERI GUARIKO DAI = "I SHALL COME"

LA LETRA "E":

EA	ADELANTE/CARAMBA	AHEAD
EKTOR(ELOTE)	EL MAIZ TIERNO PARA COMER	TENDER CORN TO EAT
EIERI(EYERI)	UN HUMANO/PERSONA	HUMAN BEING, PERSON
EMAHAGUA(EMAJAGUA)	COLOR CREMA/RUBION	CREAM COLOR, BLONDISH
ENAO	ROPA	CLOTING
ENEKEN	FIBRAS DE LA PLANTA MAGUEY USADAS PARA TEXTIL	FIBERS FROM THE MAGUEY USED FOR TEXTILE

LA LETRA "F":

FAIBANO	FUENTE DE RECURSOS	SOURCE
FAIBA	COMENSAR/EMPESAR	TO BEGIN, TO START
FAOBA	TERMINAR/COMPLETAR, EL FIN	TO END, FINISH, COMPLETE
FATULA	CUCARACHA GRANDE	LARGE ROACH
FUANA	CORAZON	HEART
FURIDI(TURSIDI)	MONTANAS DE FURGO CUBIERTAS DE NUBES O HUMO/VOLCAN	MOUNTAINS COVERED BY CLOUDS OF SMOKE, VOLCANO

LA LETRA "G"

GIA(PARA)	LLUVIA/DILUVIO	RAIN/DELUGE
GIIE GIIE	ALMA DE UN ARBOL	THE SOUL OF A TREE
GONGOLI	GUSANO CIEGO CON MUCHAS PATAS	BLIND WORM WITH MANY LEGS
GUA	ESO QUE ES SAGRADO MISTERIOSO/CULTO, ESPIRITUAL/MAGICO	THAT WHICH IS SACRED, MYSTERIOUS, OCCULT/MAGIC SPIRITUAL
GUABA	ARANA VENENOSA	POISONOUS SPIDER
GUABAIRE	FALCON DE LA NOCHE	NIGHT HAWK
GUABANSE	ATABEY EN SU ESTADO DE DESTRUCCION	ATABEY IN HER DESTRUCTIVE STATE
GUABARA	LANGOSTA DE RIO	RIVER LOBSTER
GUABARANI	CASCARA/CASCARON CONCHA/CARACOLES	SHELL
GUABINAO	CANSADO/FLOJO	TIRED/WEAK
GUAKA	ALTAR	ALTER
GUAKAR	HERMANO DE YUKIYU	YUKIYU'S BROTHER
GUAKARA	CUEVA	CAVE
GUADA(MAINA)	JARDIN	GARDEN
GUA GUA	NINO	CHILD
GUAGUANAN	OPORTUNIDAD	OPPORTUNITY
GUAGU IONA	EL MITOLOGICO ANCESTRAL HOMBRE HUMANO (ADAN)	THE MYTHICAL ANCESTRAL HUMAN MALE (ADAM)
GUAHAKA	MUSGO	MOSS
GUAI	"OH"/"OW"	"OH"/"OW"
GUAIABA	GUAYABA	GUAVA
GUAIBA	"VAMONOS"	LET'S GO, LET'S LEAVE
GUAIBBA(HUAIBA)	RETIRARSE/VETE	RETREAT/GO AWAY
GUAIBO	AUSENTE/DISTANTE	
GUAIKO	CIRCULO SAGRADO	SACRED CIRCLE
GUAILI	NINO PEQUENO/INFANTE	SMALL CHILD, INFANT
GUAITIAO(GUARIKEN)	MIRA, VEN A VER, AMIGO	LOOK, COME AND SEE, FRIEND
GUAHANA(GUAJANA)	FLOR DE CANA	SUGAR CANE FLOWER
GUAKA	REGION/CERCANIA	REGION, VICINITY
GUAKABINA	PROVISION DE VIAJE	PROVISION FOR JOURNEY
GUAKIA	NOSOTROS	WE

GUAKO	TE	TEA
GUAKOKIO	HOMBRE	MAN
GUAKONAX	ANTORCHA	TORCH
GUA KU	PODER DE LA TIERRA, MAGIA	EARTH MAGIC
GUAMA	SENORA	LORD, L...
GUAMIKENI	SENOR DE TIERRA Y AGUA	LORD O... EARTH ... WATER
GUAMIKINA	SENOR GRANDE	GREAT L...
GUAMO	CARACOL USADO PARA TROMPETEAR	SHELL U... A TRUMPE...
GUANA	PAPA	POTATO
GUANABAKOA	SITIO DE PALMAS ALTAS	PLACE OF TALL PALM TREES
GUANAHO(GUANAJO)	PAVO	TURKEY
GUANANA	GANSO/PATO	GOOSE/DUCK
GUANARA	LUGAR O SITIO APARTADO/ESCONDIDO, ENCARCELAMIENTO, CLAUSTURA	PLACE OR HIDDEN SITE, IMPRISONMENT CLOISTER
GUANARO	PALOMA	DOVE
GUANATABEI	PRIMITIVO/ALREVES, ESTUPIDO	PRIMITIVE, BACKWARD, STUPID
GUANEKE	POR QUE NOSOTROS?	WHY US?
GUANIME	BOLLITOS DE MAIZ	CORN ROLLS
GUANIN	ORO MORADO DE SEGUNDA CLASE USADO COMO JOYA Y ESTIMADO POR LA GENTE	PURPLELISH GOLD USED JEWELRY AND ESTEEM BY THE PEOPLE
GUAO	VENENOSO	POISONOUS
GUARA	SITIO/POSICIO/LUGAR	SITE/PLACE, POSITION
GUARACHA	TIPO DE CACION Y BAILE	TYPE OF SONG AND DANCE
GUARAGUAO	FALCON/SIMBOLO DEL DEL ESTE	HAWK/SYMBOL OF THE EAST
GUARAREI	LOCURA	INSANITY
GUARAREIBO	VICION	VISION
GUARES	JEMELOS	TWINS
GUARIBO	HOMBRE BRAVO	FIERCE MAN
GUARIBI	NINO	BOY
GUARIBGUAMA	SENOR	LORD
GUARICHE	HERMANA(S)/MUJER(S)	WOMEN, SISTERS
GUARICHI	NINA	GIRL
GUARIKITEN	CAMA DE PALOS Y RAMAS	BED OF STICKS AND BRANCHES
GUARIKO	HERMANOS/HOMBRES	BROTHERS/MEN
GUARISHGUAMA	PRINCESA	PRINCESS
GUASABARA	GUERRA	WAR

Taino	Español	English
GUASANAGA	DIVERTIRSE CON MUCHO RUIDO	TO ENJOY WITH LOUD SOUND
GUASIMA	ARBOL PARA HACER	TREE TO MAKE
GUASONA	VERDAD	TRUTH/TRUE
GUATA	MENTIRA	A LIE
GUATAKA	VASIJA DE HIGUERA	GOUR VASE
GUATABAKONO	PIPA/MUCHO HUMO	PIPE/MUCH SMOKE
GUATABAKO	FUMAR	TO SMOKE
GUATAKA	PRESIAR/APLAUDIR, GLORIFICAR	PRAISE, APPLAUSE, GLORIFY
GUATA UBA	SENOR DEL TRUENO Y RELAMPAGO	LORD OF THUNDER AND LIGHTNING
GUATEKE	FIESTA CON MUSICOS, BAILE Y COMIDA	FEAST/PARTY WITH FOOD DANCING & MUSICIANS
GUATU	QUEMAR/QUEMADA/FUEGO	BURN/TO BURN/FIRE
GUATU HIU	EN LLAMAS	IN FLAMES
GUATU HU	CALUROSO	WARM
GUATU HU HU	CALIENTE	HOT
GUATUKAN	VIEJO/ANTIGUO	OLD/ANCIENT
GUATUREI	LAS DEIDADES/EL COSMO, EL GRAN ESPIRITU, NATURELEZA/UNIDAD DEL COSMO	THE DIETIES, THE COSMOS, THE GREAT SPIRIT, NATURE, COSMIC UNITY
GUAI	AY!/CUIDADO	OUCH!/BE CAREFUL
GUAIABA	DIOS TAINO DE LA MUERTE	TAINO GOD OF DEATH
GUAIKA	CARATULA/MASCARA	MASK
GUAIO	RALLO	THUNDER
GUEI	EL SOL/REPRESENTADO EN FORMA DE DISCO	THE SUN, REPRESENTED IN DISC FORM
GUIRA	HIGUERA REDONDA USADA PARA HASER MARACAS	ROUND GOURD USE TO MAKE MARACAS
GUIRO	HIGUERA LARGA USADA PARA HASER GÜIROS	LONG GOURD USE TO MAKE GUIROS
GUIS	LA FUERZA DE VIDA DE ALGO VIVIENTE, LOCALIZADA EN EL EN EL CORAZON/EL ALMA	LIFE FORCE OF A LIVING THING, LOCATED IN THE HEART, THE SOUL
GUIS BARA	PLUMA/PELO VIVO	FEATHER/LIFE HAIR

LA LETRA "H":

HA	ASI/DE ESTE MODO CIERTAMENTE	THIS WAY/YEA SURELY
HABA(JABA)	BOLSA/POUCHO SAGRADO, PAUCHO MEDICINAL,	BAG/SACRED BAG/MEDICINE POUCH
	CANASTA TEJIDA SUELTAMENTE	LOOSE WEAVE BASKET
HABANO	CIGARRO	CIGAR
HABAO	BLANCO LIGADO CON NEGRO	WHITE MIXED WITH BLACK
HABUKO	BOLSA/CANASTA GRANDE	LARGE BAG, BASKET
HAGUA	GUSANO DE PALO	WOOD WORM
HAN HAN(JAN JAN)	SI/ASI SEA/AMEN	YES/LET IT BE/AMEN
HAIBA	CAMARON	SHRIMP
HAIBERIA(JAIBERIA)	ASTUCIA/MAÑA	CUNNING, BAD HABIT
HAITINAL	POSTE LARGO/SIERRA DE MONTANAS ALTAS	LONG POLE, HIGH MOUNTAIN RANGE
HAKANITO	CANSADO/VEJEZ	TIRED/OLD
HAMA	COMER	TO EAT
HAMAKA	CAMA COLGANTE	HAMMOCK
HAMAGUA	COMIDA	FOOD
HANEKE	POR QUE USTEDES?	WHY YOU?
HAOMAN	NUTRIR	NURTURE
HAR	SI	YES
HARA	AUTORIDAD/EN CONTROR, FUERZA DE VOLUNTAD, PODER SOBRE ALGO	AUTHORITY, IN CONTROL, WILL POWER, POWER OVER SOMETHING
HARA	TODO	ALL
HARANA	MUCHOS/AS	MANY
HARAIAN	MANDO/MANDAR	COMMAND
HATAKA	CUCHARA DE HIGUERA	SPOON MADE OF GOUR
HATIKO(JATIKO)	MALLA PARA LA PESCA	NET FOR FISHING
HE	RADICAL/EXTREMO	RADICAL, EXTREME
HEBA	MUJER DESHONROSA, HECHICERA MALVADA	DISHONORABLE WOMAN/EVIL, SORCERESS
HE BOGUA	CONCEPCION DE VIDA, EMBARAZO/PRENEZ	CONCEPTION OF LIFE, PREGNANCY
HEKIA	COMPLETO/CUMPLIDO	COMPLETE, ACOMPLISH

HEKEI	PRIMERO	FIRST
HEKETI	UNO/UN/O	ONE/A/AN
HEKEGUA	SOLO/DOLEDOSO	ALONE/LONELY
HEKETIN	UNION/UNIDAD, CONVERSAR	UNION/UNITY, CONVERSING
HEME	MEDIDA CON LOS DEDOS	MEASUREMENT WITH THE FINGERS
HI(HIBA,JIBA)	MONTE	WOODS
HIBARO	HOMBRE DEL MONTE	MAN OF THE MOUNTAIN
HIBE	COLADOR	STRIANER
HIBI	CANASTA PARA CERNIR ARINA	BASKET TO SIEVE GRAIN
HIBIRIA	MELON	WATERMELON
HIBITS	CANASTERIA/CERNERO	BASKETRY, SIFTER
HIGUAKA	PAPAGAYO	PARROT
HIKI	ARBOL CON MADERA DURA	TREE WITH HARD WOOD
HIKOTEA	TORTUGA	TORTOISE
HIKIHI	DISPARA	TO FIRE
HIKIRI	ARMA(ARCO,MACANA)	WEAPON
HIMAGUA	JEMELO	TWIN
HIMAGUANO	EL CONCEPTO SAGRADO DE DUALIDAD	THE SACRED OF DUALITY
HIRIGUAO(JIRIGUAO)	PIOJO	LOUSE
HOBA(JOBA)	BEBIDA DE MAIZ	CORN DRINK
HOBO BABA(IOBO BABA)	CUEVA DE DONDE SALIA EL SOL Y LA LUNA	CAVE WHERE THE SUN & THE MOON CAME OUT OF
HOHOTO(JOJOTO)	PODRIDO/DANADO	SPOILED, CORRUPT
HOKUMA	ARBOL TROPICAL	TROPICAL TREE
HU	VIENTO/ALIENTO DE DE VIDA/CONICIENTE DE VIDA	WIND/BREATH OF LIFE, AWARENESS OF LIFE
HUAMO	SOMBRA	SHADOW
HUAN	AIRE	AIR
HUANI	RESPIRAR	TO BREATH
HUARA(HUAVA)	TU	YOU
HUBA	FUERTE	STRONG
HUEI	CANGREJO DE MANGLE	JUNGLE CRAB
HUIBO	ALTO/ALTURA	HIGH, ALTITUDE
HUMA	BORRACHO/BAJO LA INFLUENCIA DE DROGAS	DRUNK/UNDER INFLUENCE OF DRUGS
HUIN	SABER/ESTAR CONCIENTE DE	TO KNOW/TO BE AWARE OF
HUPIA	REFLEXION DE UN MUERTO/ESPIRITU	REFLECTION OF THE DEAD,

	DE UN DIFUNTO	SPIRIT OF A DECEASED
HURAK<u>A</u>N(JURAK<u>A</u>N)	DIOS DE LA TORMENTA, HURACAN/TORNADO,	LORD OF THE STORM, HURRICANE, TORNADO
HUT<u>I</u>A(JUT<u>I</u>A)	UN ROEDOR COMESTIBLE DEL CARIBE	A LARGE, EDIBLE CARIBIAN RODENT

LA LETRA "I":

I<u>A</u>	QUE?	WHAT?
I<u>A</u>H	EL ALUMBRE DE VIDA	LIFE GLOW
IAD UP<u>I</u>A TE	BUSCAR/BUSCADOR	SEEK/SEEKER
IAD UP<u>I</u>A TE B<u>A</u>I	POR QUE?	WHY?
IAD UP<u>I</u>A TE H<u>A</u>RA	QUERER/DESEAR	TO WANT, TO DESIRE
IAGH<u>A</u>I	UN SER VIVIENTE	A LIVING BEING
IAGU<u>A</u>SA	PATO SILVESTRE	WILD DUCK
I<u>AI</u>A	DIOS DEL DILUVIO	GOD OF DELUGE
IAMOK<u>A</u>I	SEGUNDO	SECOND
IAMON K<u>O</u>BIRE	CUATRO	FOUR
IANABO	TRAISIONAR	BETRAYAL, TREASON
IAR<u>A</u>	LUGAR/SITIO	PLACE
IAR<u>E</u>I	CANASTA	BASKET
I<u>A</u>RI	COLLAR DEL BEIKE	BEIKE'S NECKLACE
IARIK<u>O</u>BO	COLLAR DE CARACOL	SHELL NECKLACE
IAR<u>I</u>MA	NALGAS/ANUS	BUTTOCKS, ANUS
IAR<u>O</u>KO	BOCA	MOUTH
IAT<u>I</u>	LUGAR ELEVADO	ELEVATED PLACE
I<u>A</u>UKA	MATAR	TO KILL
I<u>E</u>IA	UNO DE LOS NOMBRES DE LA MADRE DE YUKIYU	ONE OF THE NAMES OF YUKIYU'S MOTHER
I<u>E</u>N	ENVENENAR	TO POISON
I<u>E</u>RA	HICE/HACER	DID DO
I<u>E</u>RE	AS ALGO	DO SOMETHING
IERI	ARE ALGO	SHALL DO
IER<u>I</u>A	LABOR	TASK
IER<u>E</u>I	TRABAJO/PROFECION, FUNCION/ACTIVIDAD, TRABAJAR/HACER	WORK, PROFESSION, FUNCTION, ACTIVITY/TO WORK/MAKE

IER<u>E</u>N	USAR/UTILIZAR	USE/UTILIZE
IERMAGUAKAR	OTRO NOMBRE POR EL CUAL LA MADRE DE DIOS ES CONOCIDA	ANOTHER NAME BY WHICH THE MOTHER OF GOD IS KNOWN
IGU<u>A</u>KA	PAPAGAYO	PARROT
IGU<u>A</u>NA	LAGARTO LLAMADO POR TAL NOMBRE	LIZARD CALLED BY SUCH NAME
<u>I</u>KINA	UNICO(A)	UNIQUE
<u>I</u>KO	SOGA O CUERDA	ROPE OR CORD
<u>I</u>MISA	MONTANA	MOUNTAIN
INAB<u>O</u>N	RIO BUENO	GOOD RIVER
INIERI	VIEJO	OLD
INRIR<u>I</u>(KAUBABAIAEL)	PAJARO CARPINTERO	WOODPECKER
IODODALI	HERMANO	BROTHER
IRI	DOLORES MENSTRUALES	MENSTRUATION CRAMPS
<u>I</u>TA	NO SE?	DON'T KNOW?
<u>I</u>T<u>A</u>BO	PANTANO	SWAMP
I<u>U</u>	BLANCO(A)/CLARO	WHITE/CLEAR
I<u>U</u>KA	PLANTA SAGRADA DE DONDE SE EXTRAE EL PAN CASAVE	SACRED PLANT FROM WHICH IS MADE CASAVE BREAD
IUK<u>A</u>	MATAR	TO KILL
IUK<u>A</u>I<u>E</u>KE	PUEBLO/ALDEA	TOWN/VILLAGE
IUK<u>E</u>	TIERRAS BLANCAS	WHITE LANDS
IUKUB<u>I</u>A	PLANTA/FOLLAJE/ARBUSTO/MALEZA	PLANT, FOLIAGE/BUSH UNDERBRUSH
IUKUB<u>O</u>A	PECHO	CHEST
IUKUBO<u>E</u>	ESTOMAGO/BARRIGA	STOMACH BELLY
IUKUBO<u>I</u>	AREA DEL INGLE	GROIN AREA
<u>I</u>UKUB<u>O</u>	CUERPO	BODY
<u>I</u>UNKE	MONTE SAGRADO DE BORIKEN	HOLY MOUNTAIN OF BORIKEN "EL YUNKE"

LA LETRA "K":

Taíno	Español	English
KA	DE EL/DE ELLA	HIS/HERS
KABAO	MADERA/PALO	WOOD
KABO	MANO	HAND
KAGUAIA	LAGARTIGA	LIZARD
KABUIA	CORDON	CORD
KAGUAMA	TORTUGA	TURTLE
KAGUAMA GUA	PROTEJER/ESCUDAR	PROTECT SHIELD
KAGUARA	CONCHITA DE ALMEJA USADA PARA PELAR LA YUCA	SMALL CLAM USED TO PEEL YAM
KAGUASO	ESPIRITU	SPIRIT
KAGUASO	YERBA	GRASS
KAH	FUERZA	FORCE
KAHAIA(KAJAIA)	TIBURON	SHARK
KAIKA	UNA ESPECIE DE COTORRA	A KIND OF PARROT
KAIKU	ARRECIFE/DIQUE	DIKE/REEF
KAIMAN	COCODRILO	CROCODILE
KAIMATI	MALO	BAD(MALE)
KAIMATU	MALA	BAD(FEMALE)
KAIO	ISLA	ISLAND
KAIRI	MES	MONTH
KAKAO	COCOA/CHOCOLATE	COCOA CHOCOLATE
KAKIA BOSIKA	EL/ELLA RECIBIERON	HE/SHE RECEIVED
KAKIA BUSIKA	EL/ELLA ADQUIRIERON	HE/SHE ACQUIRED
KAKIAKATO	ELLA	SHE/HER
KAKIALI	EL	HE/HIM
KAKIANO	ELLOS/ELLAS	THEY
KAKONA	PEPITA DE ORO	GOLD NUGGET
KAKU(KAKO/AKO)	OJO	EYE
KAKULO	INSECTO DANINO A PLANTAS Y ARBOLES	HARMFUL INSECT TO TREES,PLANTS
KAL	ALIMENTO	NOURISHMENT
KALICHI	QUEBRADA DE AGUA DULCE	SWEET WATER BROOK
KAMUI	SOL	SUN
KANA	PALMA DE SITIO ALTO PARA CUBRIR LOS BOHIOS	PALM FOUND IN HIGH PLACES USED FOR ROOFING
KANARI	VASIJA DE BARRO PARA AGUA	CERAMIC JAR FOR WATER
KANEI	TEMPLO/HOGAR CEREMONIAL DEL JEFE	TEMPLE, CEREMONIAL HOME OF THE CHIEF
KANIBA(KARIBE)	CANIBAL	CANIBAL
KANO	DE ELLOS	THEIR'S

KANOA	CANOA/BOTE	CANOE/BOAT
KANOKUM	TRES, #3	THREE, #3
KANSI	CASA/LOGIA DE SUDAR O DE VAPOR	SWEAT LODGE/ STEAM LODGE
KAO	CHANGO	CROW
KAOBANA	CEDRO	CEDAR
KAONA	ORO COMO EL SUDOR DEL SOL/ORO SAGRADO	GOLD AS THE SWEAT OF THE SUN, SACRED GOLD
KAONAO	MONTANA DE ORO, O ORO	GOLDEN MOUNTAIN, OR GOLD
KARAI	CASTIGAR	PUNISH
KARAIAEN	LEVANTARSE/SALIR A FUERA	TO WAKE UP, TO GO OUT- SIDE
KARAKARA	ESPECIE DE FALCON QUE EXISTIO EN PUERTO RICO, TODAVIA EXISTE EN PARAGUAY & ARGENTINA	KIND OF FALCON THAT EXISTED IN PUERTO RICO, STILL EXIS- TING IN PARAGUAY & ARGENTINA
KARAKARAKOL	RONOSO(POR ENFERMEDAD EN LA PIEL)	SCABBY (BECAUSE OF SKIN ILLNESS
KARAKURI	JOYA PARA LA NARIZ	JEWEL USED ON THE NOSE
KARAO(KARAU)	ESPECIE DE AVE MUY RARA EN P.R. MIDIENDO 25 A 28 PULGADAS, VIVIENDO EN EL INTERIOR DE BOSQUES O EL YUNQUE	KIND OF BIRD VERY RARE IN P.R. MEASU- RING 25 TO 28 INCHES, LIVING IN INTERIOR OF FORESTS OR THE YUNQUE
KARATO	REFRESCO HECHO DE GUANABANA, AZUCAR Y AGUA	JUICE MADE OF GUANABA- NA, SUGAR AND WATER
KAREI	TORTUGA DE MAR	SEA TURTLE
KARIAKO	MAIZ CON TONOS ROJOS	CORN WITH RED TONES
KARRUCHO	MARISCO AFRODISIACO	APHRODISIAC SHELL FISH
KASABE	PAN ECHO DE YUCA	CASSAVA BREAD
KASAGUA	CONVOCAR/LLAMAR	SUMMON
KASIKE	JEFE	CHIEF
KATAURE	CAJA ECHA DE HOJAS	BOX MADE OF

	DE PALMA	PALM FRONDS
KATEI	UNA CLASE DE PERIQUITO PEQUENO	A KIND OF SMALL PARAKEET
KATI	NONBRE USADO EN FORMA MASCULINA	NOUN USED DENOTING MASCULINE OR MALE
KATIBIA	HARINA DE YUCA	GRAIN MADE OF YAM
KATO	NOMBRE USADO EN FORMA FEMENINA	NOUN USED DENOTING FEMALE OR FEMININE
KATONI	ANCESTRAS	FEMALE ANCESTORS
KATOTE	HIJA	DAUGHTER
KATSI(KATTI,KARAYA)	LUNA	MOON
KAURA	RAZA	RACE
KE	MUNDO/TIERRA	WORLD/EARTH
KENEPAI	FRUTA	FRUIT
KESIKE IA(KISKE IA)	ISLA DE SANTO DOMINGO	ISLAND OF SANTO DOMINGO
KIANI	LAGUNA	POND
KO	SITIO DE BUENAS TIERRAS	PLACE OF GOOD LANDS
KOA	PALO PARA PLANTAR, SINBOLO CEREMONIAL DE LA CULEBRA	DIGGING STICK, CEREMONIAL SNAKE SYMBOL
KOABAI(KOAIBAI)	TIERRA DE LOS MUERTOS, VIENTRE DE ATABEI	LAND OF THE ATABEI'S WOMB
KOAL	MUERTO	DEAD
KOATI(KOATI MUNDI)	MAPACHE	RACOON
KOATRISKIE	DIOS DE LA LLUVIA	LORD OF RAIN
KOBELA	ESPECIE DE CULEBRA GRIS O NEGRA CON CON RAYAS	KIND OF GREY OR BLACK SNAKE WITH STRIPES
KOBO	CONCHA	CONCH SHELL
KOBOSIMU	MASCARA/CARA DE CARACOL	MASK/SHELL FACE
KOBIHA	TECHO	ROOF
KOEIA(OEIA)	ESTRELLA	STAR
KOHIBA(KOJIBA)	TABACO	TABACO
KOHOBANO(KOJOBANO)	ARBOL USADO EL POLVO PARA FUMAR EN PIPA	TREE USED IN POWDER FORM TO SMOKE IN PIPES
KOHOIO	PENE	PENIS
KOHON(KOJON)	TESTICULOS	TESTICLES
KOIMA	AYUNO DE LOS BOHIKES	FASTING OF THE SHAMAN

KOKI	COQUI	SMALL TREE
KOKO	COCO	COCONUT
KOKOLIA	DOS CLASES DE CANGREJOS EL AZUL DE AGUA SALADA Y EL NEGRO DE AGUA DULCE	TWO KINDS OF CRABS THE BLUE ONE OF SALT WATER & THE BLACK ONE OF SWEET WATERS
KOKU	LUZ	LIGHT
KOKUIA	CUCUBANO	FIRE FLY
KOKUIU	GRILLO	CRICKET
KOLISIBI	COLLAR/PRENDA	NECKLACE, JEWELRY
KOMEHEN	COMEJEN	TERMITE
KONUKO	TIERRA CULTIVADA	CULTIVATED FIELD
KO OBA	RITO ECHO POR LOS LIDERES ESPIRITUALES	RITUAL MADE BY THE SHAMAN
KORAIA	REPENTIMIENTO	REPENTANCE
KORASI	MOSQUITO GRANDE	LARGE MOSQUITO
KORI	RRATON	MOUSE
KORO	RODILLA	KNEE
KOROKATO	ABUELA	GRANDMOTHER
KOROMO	ABUELA DEL OESTE	GRANDMOTHER OF THE WEST
KORUA	AVE SILVESTRE	A WILD BIRD
KOSUBA	LA TELA QUE CUBRE EL GRANO DE MAIZ	THE FILM THAT COVERS THE CORN
KOTUI	INDIVIDUO BIEN NEGRO	A VERY DARK PERSON
KOIOL	GUERRERO	WARRIOR
KOIOR	CAFE TOSTADO EN SU CASCARA	COFFEE ROASTED IN ITS SHELL
KU	SITIO SAGRADO	SACRED PLACE
KUA	RELUCIENTE/BRILLANTE	BRIGHT, SHINING
KUBA	LA MAYOR DE LAS ISLAS ANTILLAS, SIGNIFICA - "SITIO GRANDE"	THE LARGEST OF THE CARRIBEAN ISLANDS/IT ALSO MEANS "BIG PLACE"
KUEI	SITIO PARA VIVIR, PARA POBLAR	LIVING SPACE, AREA FOR SETTLING
KUISA	PALETILLA DE MADERA PARA VOLTIAR LAS TORTAS DE CASABE	SMALL WOODEN PADDLE, USE TO TURN OVER THE

		CASABE
KU_I_U	LUCERO RELUCIENTE	BRIGHT STAR
KUH_E_(KUJ_E_)	VARA FLEXIBLE	FLEXIBLE ROD
KUN_U_KU	CULTIVAR	FARMIMG
KUSUB_I_	LICOR HECHO DEL JUGO DE LA YUCA	LIQUOR MADE FROM THE JUICE OF THE YUCA
KU_I_A_I_A	NOMBRE DADO AL FALCON COMUN	NAME GIVEN TO THE COMMON FALCON

LA LETRA "L":

LAN_E_KE	?POR QUE EL?	WHY HIM?
L_E_KO	CAMA	BED
LI	EL/LA/LO/ESO(A)	IT/THAT
L_I_AN_I_	ESPOSA	WIFE
LI_E_IA(I_E_IA)	OMNIPOTENTE	OMNIPOTENT
LO_I_K_I_ANO	USTEDES	YOU(PLURAL)
LO_I_K_I_A	TU	YOU (SINGULAR)
LO_I_	TUYO/DE USTEDES	YOUR/YOURS
L_U_NA	DIOSA DE LOS PARTOS, DE LA MEDICINA	GODDESS OF DE LIVERIES, OF MEDICINE

LA LETRA "M":

MA	PREFIJO QUE SIGNIFICA "SIN/SIN TENER" EX. "MA GUANARA" "SIN ENCARSERACION" "LIBRE"	A PREFIX - "WITHOUT, LACKING" EX. "MA GUANARA" "WITHOUT ENSLAVEMENT" "FREE"
MA	GRANDE	BIG
MA_A_ITE	MELLADO/SIN DIENTES	TOOTHLESS
MA B_O_IA	ESPIRITU MALIGNO	EVIL SPIRIT
MA B_U_IA	GRAN ESPIRITU	GREAT SPIRIT
MACHAB_U_CA	?QUE ME IMPORTA?	WHAT DOES IT MATTER TO ME?
MAGU_A_	VEGA GRANGE	LARGE FERTILE PLAIN
MAGU_A_NA	VEGA PEQUENA	SMALL FERTILE PLAIN
MA GU_A_NARA	ESTAR LIBRE,	TO BE FREE,

	PERMITIR	TO ALLOW
MAGUEI	PLANTA FIBROSA DE DONDE SE HACIAN LAS HAMACAS	FIBROUS PLANT FROM WHICH HAMMOCKS WERE MADE FROM
MAHA	UN TIPO DE LA CULEBRA BOA	A TYPE OF BOA SNAKE
MAHABOA	GRACIAS/DAR GRACIAS, GRATITUD	THANK/TO THANK, GRATITUDE
MAHARA	NINGUN(A/O)	NONE
MAIAKAN	TAMBOR	DRUM
MAIANI	SILENCIO/SILENCIOSO, CALMAR(DO/DA), SERENO(A)/SUBYUGAR VENCER	QUIET, QUIETLY, CALM SERENE, SUBDUE, OVERCOME
MAILE	MELLADO/SIN DIENTES	TOOTHLES
MAIOABAU	INSTRUMENTO DE CUERDA	STRINGED INSTRUMENT
MAIOWAKAN(MAGUEI)	TAMBOR DE MADERA	WOODEN DRUM
MAISI(MAIS)	MAIS	CORN
MAHA(MAJA)	CULEBRA MUY GRANDE, SU ACEITE ES MEDICINAL	BIG SNAKE, ITS OIL IS MEDICINAL
MA KA	ARBOL ALTO	HIGH TREE
MAKANA	MACANA/HACHA	HATCHET, CLUB
MAKATARIE GUAIABA	DIOS DE LA MUERTE	GOD OF DEATH
MAKO	SAPO	TOAD
MAKORI	LENGUAJE EXTRANO	STRANGE LANGUAGE
MAKU(MAKAKO,MAACO)	SIN OJOS	WITHOUT EYES
MAKUTO	CANASTA	BASKET
MAMON	YUKIYU ABUELO DE LOS DIOSES SUPREMOS QUE GUARDA Y PRESERVA LAS TRADICIONES	YUKIYU GRANDFATHER OF THE SUPREME GODS THAT KEEPS & PRESERVES THE TRADITIONS
MAMONA	ABUELA DE LOS DIOSES SUPREMOS QUE GUARDA LA ENERGIA DE TODO SER VIVIENTE	GRANDMOTHER OF THE SUPREME GODS WHO IS KEEPER OF THE ENERGY OF ALL LIVING THINGS
MANAIA	CUCHILLO	KNIFE
MANAMA	DESESPERADO(A)	DISPAIR
MANATI	UN MAMIFERO DE MAR	A WATER MAMMAL
MANGLE	ARBOL QUE VIVE EN	TREE THAT

	LAGUNAS Y LA ORILLA DEL MAR	IN LAGOONS & AT THE SHORE OF THE OCEAN
MAN<u>I</u>	MANI	PEANUT
MAN<u>I</u>GUA	UN AREA SALVAJE, UN BOSQUE/UNA SELVA	A WILD AREA, A FOREST, A JUNGLE
MANIK<u>A</u>TO	PERSONA BUENA	GOOD PERSON
MAROH<u>O</u>	LA LUNA (PRESENTADA EN SEMI EN UNA CUEVA EN SANTO DOMINGO)	THE MOON PRESENTED AS A SEMI IN A CAVE IN DOMINICAN REPUBLIC
MARO<u>I</u>A(MARO<u>IO</u>)	LA LUNA	THE MOON
MAOROKOT<u>I</u>	DIOS	GOD
MARO<u>U</u>	TIEMPO DESPEJADO, CIELO SIN NUBES	CLEAR SKY, SKY WITHOUT CLOUDS
M<u>A</u>OTIA	MANANA	MORNING
MAPAGU<u>A</u>IA	BASIO	EMPTY
MAR<u>A</u>KA	MARACA	MARACA
MAR<u>E</u>N	EXTENSO/LLANO	VAST/PLANE
MAR<u>U</u>GA	MARACA PEQUENA	SMALL RATTLE
MAT<u>I</u>	PEQUENO	SMALL
MAT<u>I</u>NIN<u>O</u>	SIN CONTENIMIENTO MASCULINO	WITHOUT MALE FORBEARS
M<u>A</u>TO	NO	NO
MAT<u>U</u>M	GENEROSO/ABUNDANTE	GENEROUS, BOUNTIFUL
MATUNHER<u>I</u>	SUB JEFE/SEGUNDO EN MANDO	SUB CHIEF, SECOND IN COMMAND
M<u>I</u>LPA	CAMPO SEMBRADO DE MAIZ	FIELD PLANTED WITH CORN
M<u>I</u>ME	INSECTO PEQUENO	SMALL INSECT
M<u>I</u>N<u>I</u>	PEQUENA FUENTE	SMALL FOUNTAIN
MO<u>I</u>N(ONIAB<u>A</u>GUA)	SANGRE	BLOOD
M<u>U</u>	MUCHO	A LOT
MUKARO	BUO/MUCARO	OWL
M<u>U</u>KURA	CERAMICA/FLORERO, JARRO	CERAMIC/VASE PITCHER

LA LETRA "N":

NA	COSA/ALGO	THING, SOMETHING
NAANEKE	?POR QUE ELLOS(AS)?	WHY THEY?
NABOR<u>I</u>A	EL SEGUIDOR DE UN LIDER POLITICO O SOCIAL	THE FOLLOWER OF A POLITICAL OR SOCIAL

		LEADER
NAIBOA	LA FLOR DE LA YUCA USADA PARA LOS CACIQUES	THE FLOWER OF THE YUCA USED FOR THE CHIEFS
NAKA	NADA	NOTHING
NAKAN	MEDIO(DE UN SITIO)	MIDDLE(OF A PLACE)
NAGUA	TAPARRABO COMUN PARA AMBOS SEXOS	COMMON LOIN-CLOTH FOR EITHER SEX
NAHE	PALETA PARA NAVEGAR LA CANOA	CANOE PADDLE
NANEKE	?POR QUE YO?	WHY ME?
NANICHI	MI AMADA	MY BELOVED
ANIKI	ESPIRITU	SPIRIT
NARGUTI	FRASE USADA PARA FAMILIAR QUERIDO COMO LOS ABUELOS	PHRASE USED FOR A BELOVED FAMILY MEMBER LIKE THE GRANDPARENTS
NASA	TRAMPA DE CANASTA PARA PESCAR	FISHING BASKETRY TRAP
NI(ONIABO)	AGUA	WATER
NIANTI	NADA PEQUENO	NOTHING SMALL
NIGUA	PULGA	FLEA
NINO	ANCESTROS/ANCIANOS	ANCESTORS, ELDERS
NIUCHE	GUERRA EN EL AGUA	WAR IN THE WATER
NITABO	LAGUNA DE AGUA DULCE	SWEAT WATER POND
NO	SUFIJO USADO PARA CREAR FORMA PLURAL EN PALABRAS (S)	SUFIX USED FOR CREATING PLURAL FORMS IN WORDS (S)
NOPAL	TUNA	TUNA
NU	NUDO	KNOT

LA LETRA "O":

O	MONTANA	MOUNTAIN
OA	PREFIJO DENOTANDO "DE NOSOTROS"	PREFIX DENOTING "OURS"
OALO	DISTANTE/LEJOS	DISTANT/FAR
OAKAR(GUACAR)	SENOR DE LAS PRUEBAS, HERMANO JEMELO DE YOKAJU	LORD OF, TRIALS, TWIN BROTHER OF YOKAJU
OAKIA	NOSOTROS	US/WE
OIOA	ESTRELLA	STAR

OIOAGUA	CIUDADANO/MIEMBRO, DE UN GRUPO	CITIZEN, MEMBER OF A GROUP
OIODODAKATO	HERMANA	SISTER
OIODODALI	HERMANO	BROTHER
OKAMA	OYE/OIR	LISTEN/TO HEAR
O KOROTI	ANCESTRO MASCULINO, ABUELO	MALE ANCESTOR, GRANDFATHER
O KOROKATO	ANCESTRA FEMENINA, ABUELA	FEMALE ANCESTOR GRANDMOTHER
ON	AUMENTAR/MAS	INCREASE, MORE
ONIABI GUA	VAPOR	STEAM
ONIABAGUA	SANGRE	BLOOD
OPEIGUA	MIEDO	FEAR
OPERITO	MUERTO(A)/MUERTE	DEAD/DEATH
OTOAO(UTUADO)	SITIO MONTANOSO	A PLACE WITH MOUNTAINS

LA LETRA "P":

PAGUAIA	LLENO(A)	FULL
PANO	DESCUBRIR, ENCONTRAR	DISCOVER, FIND
PARA	LLUVIA	RAIN
PEITIKAKO	OJOS NEGROS, EXPRECION OFENSIVA ENTRE LOS INDIOS	BLACK EYES, OFFENSIVE. EXPRESSION AMONG THE INDIANS
PIRAGUA	EMBARCACION MAYOR DE CANOA	A MAJOR CANOE EMBARKATION
PITIRRE	PAJARO COLOR GRIS ENCIMA Y ANARANJADO POR DE BAJO DEL CARIBE	BIRD WITH GREY FEATHERS ON TOP & ORANGE FEATHERS AT THE BOTTOM FOUND IN THE CARRIBEAN
PU	COLOR ROJO	COLOR RED
PUAIA	VENGANSA/VENGAR	REVENGE, AVENGE

LA LETRA "R":

RA	LUGAR DE NACIMIENTO	PLACE OF BIRTH
RAHUA	FRESCO	FRESH

RAIS	PUNZAR	PIERCE
RAKAN	FUERZA/PODER	STRENGTH, POWER
RAKUNO	ABUELA DEL DEL NORTE	GRANDMOTHER OF THE NORTH
RANA	PASADO	PAST
RAO	ESTABILIDAD/BALANCIA, FIRMESA	STABILITY, BALANCE, FIRMNESS
RAO BUSIKA	REGALO/CUALIDAD, ATRIBUTO	GIFT/QUALITY ATTRIBUTE
RAONA	GUIAR/CONDUCIR	GUIDE/LEAD
RAOBA	OTRO(A)	OTHER
RAREI	SUENO	DREAM
RENE	PRERSENTE	PRESENT
RINIAO	JOVEN/NUEVO(A)	YOUNG/NEW
RO	AMOR/QUERES	LOVE/TO LOVE
ROKO	CONOCER	TO KNOW

LA LETRA "S":

SABANA	LLANURA GRANDE	LARGE PLAIN
SAKI	BIEN/BUENO(A)/MEJOR	FINE/GOOD WELL
SAKIA	BELLEZA	BEAUTY
SAKI ASI	SABIDURIA	WISDOM
SAKI GUA	AMOR	LOVE
SAEN	COMPARTIR	TO SHARE
SAEN KI	JUSTICIA	JUSTICE
SANANO(SANAKO)	BOBO	DUM
SAOBAN	SUERTE/FORTUNA	LUCK/FORTUNE
SAO	DIFICULTAD	DIFICULTY
SAROBEI(SOROBEI)	ALGODON	COTTON
SASABI(XAXABI)	COTORRA	MACAW
SAU SAU	PAN DELGADO	THIN BREAD
SEITI(PEITI)	COLOR NEGRO	BLACK COLOR
SEMI	UNA FUERZA SUPER-NATURAL CON IDENTIDAD ESPECIFICA/UN ESPIRITU NATIVO/PRESENTADO ALGUNAS VECES EN FORMA TRIANGULAR	SUPERNATURAL FORCE WITH A SPECIFIC IDENTITY/A NATIVE SPIRIT/PRESENTED MANY TIMES IN TRIANGULAR SHAPE
SEMIL	DOS COSAS UNIDAS, EMPAREJADAS	TWO THINGS JOINED, ABREAST
SEMI SAKI	ESPIRITU GUARDIAN	GUARDIAN SPIRIT
SENECO	ABUNDANTE	ABUNDANT
SERENO	ROCIO DE LA MANANA	MORNING DEW
SERRA	CAMBIO/CAMBIAR	TO EXCHANGE
SETI	PEZ CHIQUITO	SMALL FISH
IANI	MUJER CASADA/ESPOSA	MARRIED, WOMAN/WIFE
SIBA	PIEDRA	STONE
SIBA BO	PIEDRA GRANDE, PEDREJON	LARGE STONE, BOULDER
SIBANA	PEDREGOSO	STONY
SIBANAKAN	MUCHAS PIEDRAS	MANY STONES
SIBAO	MONTANA DE PIEDRA	STONE MOUNTAIN
SIBUKAN	BOLSA USADA PARA ESPRIMIR LA YUCA Y HACER CASABE	BAG USED TO SQUEEZE THE YUCA & MAKE CASABE
SIERI	NARIZ	NOSE
SIEVA	MOSCA	FLY
SIGARE	SIGARRO	CIGAR
SIGUA	CARACOL	SNAIL
SIMARO	FLECHA	ARROW
SIMU	CARA/FRENTE,	FACE/FRONT,

SINA	PRINCIPIO	BEGINNING
SINAO	IRA	RAGE
SINATU	ENFERMEDAD	SICKNESS
	IRRITADO/ERIDO, DOLOR/PONERSE INFLAMADO	IRRITATED, HURT/PAIN, BECOME SORE
SINATUPARA	LLORAR	CRY/WEEP
SIPEI	BARRO PEGAJOSO	STICKY CLAY
SOBAIKO	ABUELA DEL ESTE	GRANDMOTHER OF THE EAST
SOBAOKO	COSTILLAS/AXILA	RIBS/ARMPIT
SOBERAO	EL PISO	THE FLOOR
SOIA	VALLE	VALLEY
SOKO	POSTES USADOS PARA SOSTENER LA CASA, UN PILAR	POLES USED FOR SUPPORTING A HOUSE A PILLAR
SOKOATA	EL POSTE MAYOR PARA SOSTENER LA CASA	THE MAIN POLE TO SUPPORT THE HOUSE
SOR	LA TARDE	AFTERNOON
SORUKA	CONMOCION ENTRE PERSONAS	UPROAR AMONG PEOPLE
SPANA	HOJA	LEAF
SUANIA	TIERRA FIRME	FIRM GROUND
SUBURUKO	MALEZA	THICKET
SUMAIKO	NOMBRE DADO A ATABEY	NAME GIVEN TO ATABEY

LA LETRA "T":

TA	Y/MAS	AND/PLUS
TABAKO	TABACO	TABACO
TABOINA	LUZ/ALUMBRAR, BRILLAR/CENTELLEANTE	LIGHT/GLOW, SHINE, SPARKLE
TABONUKO	INCIENSO EXTRAIDO DE TAL ARBOL	INCENSE EXTRACTED FROM SUCH TREE
TABUKO	CIGARRO	CIGAR
TADI	A	TO
TAGUAGUA	JOYA DE ORO USADA PARA ADORNARSE	GOLD JEWEL USED FOR DECORATION
TAI	LA ESENCIA DESEADA DE TODA PERSONA O SOCIEDAD PAZ/HONOR, JUSTICIA/ETC.	THE ESSENCE DESIRED OF A PERSON OR SOCIETY, PEACE/HONOR, JUSTICE/ETC.
TAIBO	AYUDAR/ASISTIR,	TO HELP/TO

	SALVAR/RESCATAR	AID/SAVE, RESCUE
TAIGS	MANDAR/ENVIAR	TO SEND
TAIN	PARA	FOR
TAINO	TODO APRECIO, HONOR PAZ SEA TUYA (USADO COMO SALUDO)	ALL PRAISE, HONOR, PEACE BE YOURS, (USED AS A GREETING)
TAIS	DE	FROM
TAKATONI	ANCESTRA	FEMALE ANCESTOR
TAN	DE	OF
TANO	TAMBIEN	ALSO
TANAMA	MARIPOSA	BUTTERFLY
TANAMO	SERCA/SERCA D	NEAR/NEAR TO

BIBLIOGRAPHY

Brau, S. (1881). <u>La colonización de puerto rico</u> (5th ed.). San Juan, Puerto Rico: Institute of Puerto Rican Culture.

Cardona Bonet, W.A. (1817). "Milicias urbanas, villa de san german" (Caja 552). Serie: Municipalidades - San German. Archivo General de Puerto Rico, Fondo Gobernadores Españoles.

Coll y Toste, C. (1972). <u>Clásicos de puerto rico</u> (2nd ed.) San Juan, Puerto Rico: Ediciones Latinoamericanas, S.A.

Hernández Aquino, L. (1977). <u>Diccionario de voces indígenas de puerto rico</u> (2nd ed.). Río Piedras, Puerto Rico: Imprime Artes Gráficas Encinas.

Granberry, J. (2004). <u>Languages of the pre-columbian antilles</u>. Tuscaloosa, Alabama: The University of Alabama Press.

Morrow Porrata, R.D. (2020). <u>Keeping the taino language alive; advanced studies in taino syntax</u>. Isabela, Puerto Rico: Yukibo Books.

Morrow Porrata, R.D. (2018). <u>Taino genealogy and revitalization</u>. Isabela, Puerto Rico: Yukibo Books.

More Books by Richard Porrata

English Version

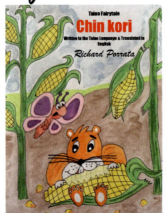

The first book written in the Taino language. This fun and exciting book tells the story of Chin kori, a mischievous little guinea pig boy who learns the hard way! This is an excellent book for both adults and children who want to learn an American Indian language. Also excellent for teachers of bilingual studies at any grade level.

Versión En Español

El primer libro escrito en lengua taína. ¡Este divertido y emocionante libro cuenta la historia de Chin kori, un niño travieso de conejillo de indias que aprende por las malas! Este es un excelente libro para adultos y niños que desean aprender un idioma indio americano. También es excelente para maestros de estudios bilingües en cualquier nivel de grado.

Versión En Español Próximamente!
Spanish Version Coming Soon!

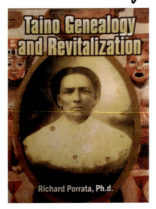

An excellent book for those of Taino ancestry who want to bolster their American Indian heritage through genealogy. This book will teach a person the methods to use in their research in order to trace a Taino ancestry using not only DNA evidence but also along with vital statistics, church records, and ancient ceramics. This book is packed full of colorful photos, ancient maps, and newly discovered history of the Caribbean found in the archives of Puerto Rico.

Preschool Science Coloring Book

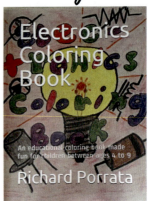

Excellent coloring book that gets toddlers from preschool through third grade interested in science through electronics. A low investment toward a bright future for a child!

All books found on amazon.com or in some books stores throughout Puerto Rico. Also check out www.yukibobooks.com

Made in United States
Orlando, FL
18 September 2023

37032858R00022